ANIMAL SAFARI

Zebras

by Derek Zobel

BELLWETHER MEDIA • MINNEAPOLIS, MN

Note to Librarians, Teachers, and Parents:

Blastoff! Readers are carefully developed by literacy experts and combine standards-based content with developmentally appropriate text.

Level 1 provides the most support through repetition of high-frequency words, light text, predictable sentence patterns, and strong visual support.

Level 2 offers early readers a bit more challenge through varied simple sentences, increased text load, and less repetition of high-frequency words.

Level 3 advances early-fluent readers toward fluency through increased text and concept load, less reliance on visuals, longer sentences, and more literary language.

Level 4 builds reading stamina by providing more text per page, increased use of punctuation, greater variation in sentence patterns, and increasingly challenging vocabulary.

Level 5 encourages children to move from "learning to read" to "reading to learn" by providing even more text, varied writing styles, and less familiar topics.

Whichever book is right for your reader, Blastoff! Readers are the perfect books to build confidence and encourage a love of reading that will last a lifetime!

This edition first published in 2012 by Bellwether Media, Inc.

No part of this publication may be reproduced in whole or in part without written permission of the publisher. For information regarding permission, write to Bellwether Media, Inc., Attention: Permissions Department, 5357 Penn Avenue South, Minneapolis, MN 55419.

Library of Congress Cataloging-in-Publication Data
Zobel, Derek, 1983-
Zebras / by Derek Zobel.
    p. cm. – (Blastoff! readers. Animal safari)
Includes bibliographical references and index.
Summary: "Developed by literacy experts for students in kindergarten through grade three, this book introduces zebras to young readers through leveled text and related photos"–Provided by publisher.
ISBN 978-1-60014-611-4 (hardcover : alk. paper)
1. Zebras-Juvenile literature. I. Title.
QL737.U62Z63 2011
599.665'7–dc22   2011005612

Printed in the United States of America, North Mankato, MN.

080111   1187

Contents

What Are Zebras?

Zebras are animals with black and white stripes. They are **related** to horses.

Every zebra has a different **pattern** of stripes.

What Zebras Eat

Zebras live and **graze** on **savannahs**. They eat grass, twigs, and bark.

Families and Herds

Male zebras are called stallions. Females are called mares. Young are called foals.

Zebras live together in families. Many families travel together in a **herd**.

One herd can have thousands of zebras. **Predators** will not attack a zebra in a herd.

A zebra family
stands in a circle if
a predator attacks.
The foals stay
inside the circle.

Grooming and Teeth

Zebras **groom** each other. They nibble each other with their teeth.

Zebras also
show their teeth to
greet each other.
Smile zebra!

Glossary

graze—to feed on grasses

groom—to clean

herd—a group of zebras that travels together; a zebra herd can have thousands of zebras.

pattern—colors or marks that repeat

predators—animals that hunt other animals for food

related—from the same animal family

savannahs—grasslands with very few trees

To Learn More

AT THE LIBRARY

Anderson, Jill. *Zebras*. Minnetonka, Minn.: NorthWord, 2005.

Fontes, Justine and Robert Fontes. *How the Zebra Got Its Stripes*. New York, N.Y.: Golden Books Family Entertainment, 2002.

Swinburne, Stephen R. *Lots and Lots of Zebra Stripes: Patterns in Nature*. Honesdale, Pa.: Boyds Mill Press, 2002.

ON THE WEB

Learning more about zebras is as easy as 1, 2, 3.

1. Go to www.factsurfer.com.

2. Enter "zebras" into the search box.

3. Click the "Surf" button and you will see a list of related Web sites.

With factsurfer.com, finding more information is just a click away.

Index

The images in this book are reproduced through the courtesy of: Eric Isselée, front cover; Mogens Trolle, pp. 5, 17; Henry Wilson, pp. 7, 9; Mitsuyoshi Tatematsu / Minden Pictures, p. 11; Yva Momatiuk & John Eastcott / Minden Pictures, p. 13; Photodisc / Photolibrary, p. 15; Elliot Neep / Masterfile, p. 19; Four Oaks, p. 21.